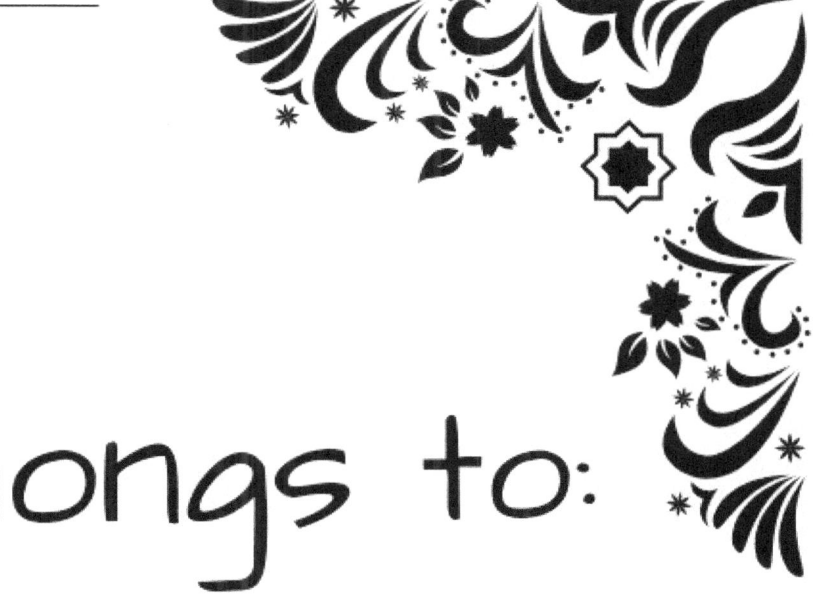

Belongs to:

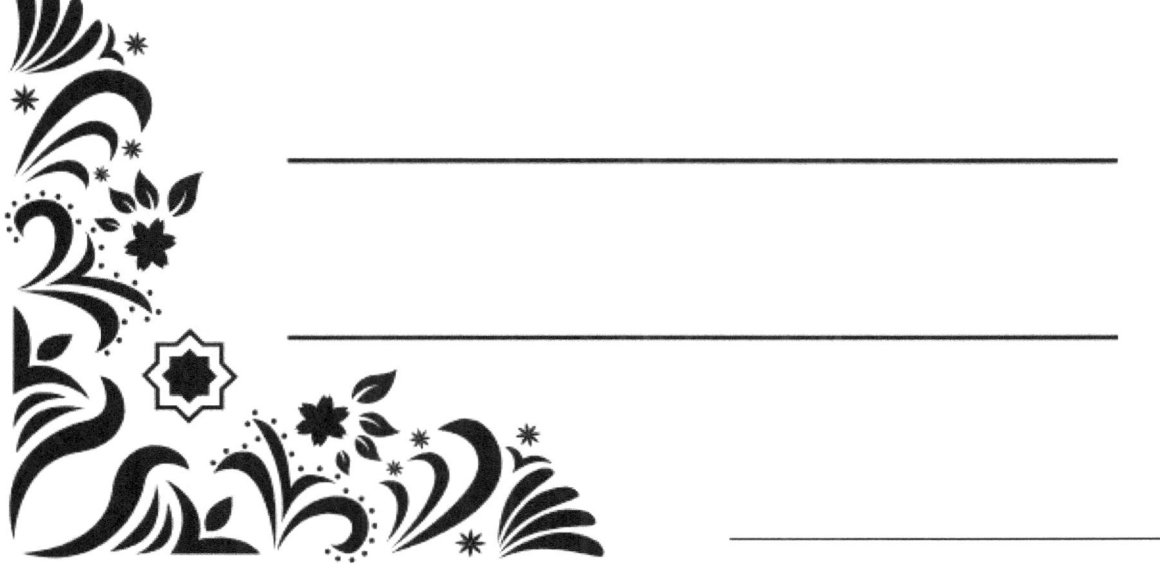

_____

_____

Title:

Title:

Title:

Title:

Title:

Title:

Title:

Title:

Title:

Title:

Title:

Title:

Title:

Title:

Title:

Title:

Title:

Title:

Title:

Title:

Title:

Title:

Title:

Title:

Title:

Title:

Title:

Title:

Title:

Title:

Title:

Title:

Title:

Title:

Title:

Title:

Title:

Title:

Title:

Title:

Title:

Title:

Title:

Title:

Title:

Title:

Title:

Title:

Title:

Title:

Title:

Title:

Title:

Title:

Title:

Title:

Title:

Title:

Title:

Title:

Title:

Title:

Title:

Title:

Title:

Title:

Title:

Title:

Title:

Title:

Title:

Title:

Title:

Title:

Title:

Title:

Title:

Title:

Title:

Title:

Title:

Title:

Title:

Title:

Title:

Title:

Title:

Title:

Title:

Title:

Title:

Title:

Title:

Title:

Title:

Title:

Title:

Title:

Title:

Title:

Title:

Title:

Title:

Title:

Title:

Title:

Title:

Title:

Title:

Title:

Title:

Title:

Title:

Title:

Title:

Title:

Title:

Title:

Title:

www.ingramcontent.com/pod-product-compliance
Lightning Source LLC
Chambersburg PA
CBHW052036280526
45791CB00010B/2984